Ye Yucky MIDDLE AGES

YE CASTLE STINKETH

Could You Survive Living in a Castle?

Chana Stiefel

Illustrated by Gerald Kelley

E Enslow Publishers, Inc.

40 Industrial Road
Box 398
Berkeley Heights, NJ 07922
USA

http://www.enslow.com

Library of Congress Cataloging-in-Publication Data

Stiefel, Chana, 1968–
    Ye castle stinketh : could you survive living in a castle? / by Chana Stiefel.
       p. cm. — (Ye yucky Middle Ages)
    Includes index.
    ISBN 978-0-7660-3786-1
    1. Castles—Juvenile literature. 2. Middle Ages—Juvenile literature. 3. Civilization,
Medieval—Juvenile literature. 4. Europe—Social life and customs—Juvenile literature.
    I. Title.
    GT3550.S86 2011
    940.1—dc22   2010019742

Paperback ISBN 978-1-59845-374-4

Printed in China

052011 Leo Paper Group, Heshan City, Guangdong, China

10 9 8 7 6 5 4 3 2 1

To Our Readers: We have done our best to make sure all Internet Addresses in this book were active and appropriate when we went to press. However, the author and the publisher have no control over and assume no liability for the material available on those Internet sites or on other Web sites they may link to. Any comments or suggestions can be sent by e-mail to comments@enslow.com or to the address on the back cover.

Illustration Credits: © 2010 Gerald Kelley, www.geraldkelley.com

Cover Illustration: © 2010 Gerald Kelley, www.geraldkelley.com

Contents

When Cows Fly

Zing! An arrow whizzes by your helmet. You duck down at your guard post on top of the castle. When all is clear . . . *fling!* You fire arrows back at the enemy below. It's been three months since those lousy invaders surrounded the castle. Food and supplies are running low. Suddenly, something big and dark is flying over your head. Is it a huge rock? No, it has legs! Holy cow . . . it's a flying cow! Those crazy enemy soldiers have launched a dead animal over the castle walls. The stinky beast lands with a splat in the castle courtyard. The stench of rotting flesh rises up to your post. *P.U.!* Now you've seen—and smelled—it all.

This isn't what you had expected when you joined the castle guard. You were hoping for good food, a warm bed, and fancy parties. Instead you're starving, sleeping on a straw mat crawling with fleas, and dodging four-legged missiles.

Want to find out what real life was like inside a medieval castle? Hold your nose and step inside!

Built for Defense

Castles were homes for the rich. They were also symbols of power. They were made to keep enemies out. The first castles, built around the year 1000 A.D., were made of wood. There was a problem, though: Attackers could burn wooden castles to the ground. The wood could also rot away. By the 1200s, castles were made of stone.

Stone castles came in all shapes and sizes. They were often surrounded by **moats**, deep ditches sometimes filled with water. Moats helped stop enemies from reaching the castle walls. Water-filled moats were also used as garbage dumps. **Sewage** often emptied into a moat. A moat formed a smelly circle around a castle. Enemy soldiers would think twice before swimming across.

6

The only way over the murky moat was to cross a bridge.
Some castles had a **drawbridge**. This wooden platform could
be used by people who lived in the castle for easy access.
It could also be slid back or raised up with chains when an
enemy attacked. If soldiers made it across, they then had to get

through the **gatehouse**. This was the guarded entry to the castle. The gatehouse was protected inside and outside the castle by two gates made of iron and wood. The gates could be raised and lowered like a trap.

Heads up! **Murder holes** were cut into the roof of the gatehouse. Defenders might drop boiling liquids, skull-crushing stones, and other missiles through these holes. If fire broke out in the gatehouse, soldiers could also pour water down the holes to put it out.

What if enemies couldn't get through the gates? They would try climbing over, breaking through, or tunneling under the castle's huge walls. (Sometimes they had to fill in the moat first.) Some castles had added rings of stone walls for extra protection. A typical outer wall was ten feet thick and forty feet high. The walls had walkways along the top,

where defenders would stand and fire their weapons. Some castles had ledges jutting out of the walls. These weren't romantic balconies like those you see in fairy tales.

8

They had holes in the floor. Soldiers could drop rocks, red-hot sand, or boiling water onto the attackers below.

The location of a castle was key. Most castles were built high on hilltops or rocky cliffs. A steep slope would be hard for an enemy to climb. Castle towers were used as lookouts. During an attack, arrows rained down from the castle walls

The Rise of Castles

Castles were built during a period in history known as the Middle Ages. These were often violent times. People fought each other over land. The more land you owned, the more power you held. Kings granted land to lords. In exchange, lords swore to fight for the king. Kings and lords often built a castle on their land. Some of them owned several castles. Owning a castle meant control of the land around the castle *and* the people who lived there. A castle was also like an army base. It was a place from which a lord could launch attacks on the enemy.

like a shower of small spears. Some castle walls were topped with ridges that looked like giants' teeth. Archers would duck behind them to escape enemy fire. Then they would fire arrows through **crenels**, the gaps between the teeth. Lower on the walls were narrow slits called **arrow loops**. Soldiers inside the castle fired arrows through these openings, too. The shower of arrows was deadly.

A castle's high ground sometimes made getting water supplies a challenge. Many castles were built near rivers. People rarely drank river water, though. It was often polluted by sewage and other wastes that were dumped into the river. River water was mostly used for cooking, bathing, and feeding animals. Down by the river, workers would fill up "waterskins." These were waterproof sacks made of animal skin. The waterskins were loaded onto the backs of horses and mules. The animals carted the water up to the castle. During a siege, this water supply could be cut off by the enemy. Many people also dug deep wells inside their castle's walls as another source of water.

Lifestyles of the Rich and Stinky

Castles weren't always at war. When residents weren't defending the castle (which was most of the time), they were busy with the chores of daily life. They also had to save up supplies in case of an attack. From food to weapons, almost everything needed during wartime or peacetime was produced by the castle. Crops were grown outside the castle walls. Poor peasant farmers grew grain, fruit, and vegetables. Their job was intense. If the crops failed, people could go hungry.

Inside the walls, castles bustled like small towns. As many as three hundred people lived and worked there. Try to imagine the sights, sounds, and smells in a busy castle: Follow your nose to the stinky stables. Here the lord's horses are cared for. Cover your ears! The smiths (metal workers) make loud, clanging noises. They're making tools, nails, and horseshoes. They're also repairing armor and weapons. A fletcher is busy making sharp arrows.

Shield your eyes from sawdust as you pass the carpenters. They are sawing boards for shields, furniture, doors, floors, and wheels. As you walk by the laundry ladies, avoid waking the sleeping soldiers. They're trying to rest after a night of guard duty.

13

Feeling hungry? Pigeons are being raised for a tender, juicy meal. Stand clear of the hot-tempered cook in the kitchen. He's busy shouting orders at young boys. They are roasting a freshly killed deer over open flames. If you're in the mood for something else, maybe you could catch a trout in the castle's fishpond. Or head over to the bakery. Fresh bread is baking on the hot floor of a fireplace. Try not to trip over the chickens pecking away at fallen grain. You can also pick fresh fruits or vegetables in the orchard and garden. While you're there,

Dark Dungeons

Some castles had hidden underground rooms. They were dark, damp dungeons. They mostly were used as storage cellars, not jails. In rare instances, prisoners were held in dungeons. These cellars were infested with creepy-crawlies. Some castles had a room called an *oubliette*, French for "forgotten room." Some prisoners were thrown into this cramped cell. They were often forgotten by the outside world. Sometimes people would look down on the prisoners through an opening above the cell.

snip some herbs for medicine. Drop them off at the "hospital," a dark room where the sick and injured stay.

Don't drink water from the well! It may be polluted. Most people in the castle drink watered down wine or a weak beer called ale. You can find some brewing at the brewhouse. Hunting dogs are barking in the kennels. Hawks and falcons, also used for hunting, are squawking in their house. Above all this noise, you might hear the sounds of farm animals. By day, cattle, sheep, and pigs are grazing in the fields—that is, if they're not being killed for dinner. At night or during battles, the animals join the rest of the crew inside the castle walls. Amidst the chaos, a prayer service is being held at a chapel. Keep in mind, all of this action is packed into an area roughly the length of a football field!

Smoky Spaces, Gloomy Rooms

When you enter the main tower of the castle, the first thing that might hit you is the smell of smoke. Castles used charcoal or wood-burning fireplaces for heat and for cooking.

Some castles had earthenware vents on top of their roofs. The vents were shaped like knights, kings, or priests. Smoke poured out of their eyes, mouths, and the tops of their heads!

In the first castles, hearths or fire pits were built in the center of the main hall. Picture a barbecue pit in the middle of your house! The central location prevented the fire from burning down the wooden walls. Drafts blowing through the castle most likely prevented the buildup of carbon monoxide, a deadly gas. Eventually, in stone castles, hearths were moved to the outer walls. They were connected to chimneys. Kitchens were moved to separate buildings to prevent fire from spreading.

After choking on the smoke, the next thing you might notice is the gloomy darkness. Electric lightbulbs weren't invented until

the 1800s. The main source of light in castles was sunlight streaming through windows. Many of the windows were small. Narrow windows meant little light, but their small size had a plus: They made it easier to defend the castle. Glass was available, but it was expensive. Open windows would let in wind, rain, and an icy chill. Wooden shutters covered the windows. Yet that left the castle in darkness.

With little sunlight, castle dwellers turned to fire to light up their homes. They often used candles. Most candles were made from globs of hardened animal fat. These candles spewed smoke. They smelled like burning, spoiled lard. Oil lamps that burned liquid animal fat were also smelly. In wealthier households, these were replaced with lamps that cleanly burned olive oil or high-priced whale oil. Beeswax candles were also pricey. They were saved for churches and the richest castles.

Chandeliers that held many candles were used to light up large rooms. During parties a castle might use a thousand candles per night. The problem was that they were a huge fire hazard. Many villages required citizens to put out the flames at night. Bells would toll after sunset to let people know when it was time to *couvre-feu*. That's French for "cover the fire." This is the origin of the modern word "curfew." Both terms have the same effect: They mean early to bed!

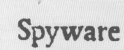

Spyware

Sometimes the walls or floors of the lord's room had squints. These were peepholes through which the lord could spy on other people in the castle.

The Great Hall

The center of action in a castle was the Great Hall. This was a large room with a high ceiling. The lord used this space for business and for entertaining guests. Meals were served in the Great Hall. The room was also used as a court of law.

The floors of the Great Hall were made of hard-packed earth or wood. Erasmus, a Dutch scholar in the fifteenth century, said castle floors were "an ancient collection of beer, grease, fragments, bones, spittle, excrement [poop] of dogs and cats, and everything that is nasty." To cover the filth, layers of straw were strewn across the floors. Sweet-smelling herbs such as lavender and mint, were scattered to cover nasty odors.

At night, the Great Hall was turned into a giant dorm room. Castle dwellers slept on itchy straw mattresses. Some snoozed on the filthy floor. Others slept on tables or benches. Fleas and lice crawled all over them. Cats chased the mice and rats that scurried about. In many castles the lord slept in a room off the Great Hall. It was separated by a curtain.

In later castles, the lord and his family had their own private bedrooms. Their beds had fluffy feather mattresses, quilts, and fur blankets. But they were crawling with bugs too. One way to chase away insects was to spread a smelly liquid, such as turpentine, on a piece of flat, stale bread. Then a candle was lit in the middle of the bread. The smell would keep bugs away.

Bath Time!

The lord and lady of the castle liked to be well groomed. Yet bathing during the Middle Ages could be a major chore. Perhaps that's why many people bathed only once a week! During warm months most people washed themselves in lakes, ponds, or streams. In the winter they bathed indoors. People in villages shared public bathhouses. Poor peasants bathed in open barrels filled with boiled water. A whole family would use the same bath water.

In castles, nobles bathed in large wooden tubs. The water was heated over a fire in the kitchen or Great Hall. Then it was hauled in big buckets to fill the tubs. In winter, lords bathed near the fireplace. The bathtubs sometimes had a fabric tent for privacy and

warmth. In warm weather, tubs were sometimes placed in the garden. A padded fabric liner in the tub prevented bathers from getting nasty splinters in their royal rear ends. Soap was made from olive oil, animal fats, or fish oil. Between baths, people would sometimes wash only their feet or hair to keep clean. It was common for people to pick lice off each other! People also didn't change and wash clothing as often as we do today. Many people only had one or two changes of clothes.

No Toilets in the Twenty-First Century? That Stinks!

Do you think people today have better sanitation than they did during the Middle Ages? Think again. Four out of ten people in the world today do not have access to a toilet. That number includes 980 million children without a clean place to poop.

Royal Toilets

Toilets in castles were called *garderobes*. This word is French for "clothes closet." There are tales that people kept clothes in these stinky rooms because the odor kept moths away. The toilets of the time were hard wooden planks with holes cut into them. The planks were held up with stone supports.

There was no toilet paper. Most people
used itchy handfuls of hay
or a curved stick called a gomphus.

Garderobes were usually built into
the thick outer walls of a castle. The waste would run down
quickly through "poop chutes" leading out of the castle. Some
toilets emptied into a moat or a river. Other toilets drained
into a **cesspit**. This deep ditch was lined with wood or stone.
It collected human waste. Cesspits allowed liquids to seep into
the ground. Solid wastes piled up in the pit. Men called gong
farmers were the sanitation crew of the Middle Ages. They had
the stinky job of digging out and hauling away the sewage from
the cesspits. Because their job was so nasty, gong farmers were
only allowed to work at night.

The richest nobles had private garderobes next to their
bedrooms. Sometimes garderobes were placed near fireplaces.
The heat provided some warmth to bare bottoms during
winter. Garderobes may also have shared a vent with a castle's
chimney. Foul fumes could be drawn up and out of the castle.
Yet there's a strong chance that the smell of sewage spread
through the castle, especially in hot weather or during a siege.

3

Feasts and Folly

Castle dwellers liked to party. Lords hosted huge feasts to impress their guests. It took a lot of food to feed a castle. Some lords spent so much money on feasts that they went broke!

In the Great Hall, servants would carry out a parade of bizarre dishes. Almost anything that could walk, crawl, fly, slither, or swim was eaten. On the royal menu were whales, porpoises, walruses, seals, and beavers. Swans and peacocks were also a delight. The cooked birds were dressed up in their own feathers. They were served in lifelike poses. Sometimes the head of a rooster was sewn onto the body of a baby pig (or the other way around)!

People enjoyed eating every part of the animal. Cooks whipped up "fancy" dishes using animal brains, livers, hearts, lungs, guts, necks, feet, and buttocks. Calves' feet were boiled to make gelatins. Like Jell-O™, these wiggly jellies were dyed bright colors. Cooked fish would "swim" in blue gelatin that was meant to look like the sea. Meat was also painted rainbow colors, such as green, blue, red, and purple.

Pies were very popular. We're not talking Grandma's apple pie. Kings would love to dig into a pie filled with mushy freshwater eels called lampreys. Another type of pie (made famous in a nursery rhyme) was filled with live blackbirds. When the king or lord cut into the pie, the birds would fly free.

Fun and Games

In the Middle Ages, there were no movies, TVs, or computers to entertain people. Jugglers, musicians, and poets entertained guests during feasts. When the tables were cleared, people would dance in circles. Then adults would play all kinds of games. Some of these games seem childlike or even violent today. In a game called Hot Cockles, one player was blindfolded and kneeled on the floor. He was then hit by the other players. He had to guess who had struck him.

Some activities were downright cruel. In a game called Bear Baiting, people would bet on a fight between a bear and a pack of wild dogs.

The most violent and dangerous competitions hosted by a castle were tournaments, or mock battles. In **melees**, teams of knights on horseback would charge at each other with long wooden spears called **lances**. They would try to knock each other off their saddles. The last knight mounted was declared the winner. Sometimes melees were just as bloody as real battles.

In a **joust**, two knights would charge against each other. They would try to knock each other off their horses. A knight also scored points by breaking his lance against his opponent's shield. Knights wore heavy armor for protection. Yet many jousts ended with injuries or even in death. Many knights refused to give up these contests. They were good practice for real battles. Knights also won riches and fame at these events. Eventually, safety measures were added. These included blunted weapons and a wall dividing the jousting knights.

31

4

Surviving a Siege

One of the greatest threats to a castle was a siege. Enemy troops would surround the castle. They blocked food and supplies. Sometimes they would poison the well water. The strategy was to starve the castle dwellers or to force them to surrender.

A siege could last for months. The castle would store lots of food in storerooms. The problem was that much of the food would rot or become moldy over time. Mice and rats raided the supplies too. Sometimes starving people ate the rodents, as well as horses, dogs, and grass.

33

Other problems developed. Castles sometimes became overcrowded with hundreds or thousands of peasants and villagers. Toilets became clogged and overflowed with sewage. Disease could spread through a castle. Food supplies could run out. In 1136, Exeter Castle in England surrendered after a three-month siege. Its well water had dried up from overuse.

Savage Siege

Between 1203 and 1204, King Philip II of France led a siege on a castle called Chateau Gaillard. As many as 2,200 villagers took shelter inside the castle. When food started to run low, Roger de Lacy, the English knight in charge of defending the castle, starting kicking out the villagers. They were considered "useless mouths" to feed. The first few hundred villagers were allowed to escape through enemy lines. However, when King Philip found out, he was furious. He wanted to drain the castle's supplies. With spears and arrows, he and his army forced the next round of escaping villagers—as many as 1,200 people—back to the castle. But the castle gates were locked. The starving, unarmed people were caught in the crossfire. For three horrible winter months, they suffered at the base of the castle. More than half of them died of hunger. Eventually, King Philip had pity on them. He gave them bread and let them pass.

Some castles were better prepared for battle. In 1299, Stirling Castle in Scotland held out against attackers for almost a year. (After all that time, you can bet that the castle smelled pretty awful from rotting garbage, sewage, and stinky soldiers!) If a castle was well stocked, the invading army could run out of supplies first.

Furious Fight

Of course, a castle wouldn't give up without a fight. For every kind of attack, the castle's defenders had a way to fight back.

Sometimes the enemy would try to scale the castle walls on ladders. Using forked poles, castle soldiers would throw down the ladders, along with the screaming climbers. Enemy hands or heads that did reach the top of the wall could be chopped off.

Carpenters for the enemy would build a **belfry**. This was a huge wooden tower the same height as the castle walls. Enemy soldiers would then fill in the castle's moat with gravel and rocks. After being loaded with troops, the belfry would be wheeled up against the castle. The soldiers would cross the belfry's bridge onto the castle walls. Armed with swords, castle knights were waiting. A bloody man-to-man fight would follow.

One belfry used in 1266 during a siege at Kenilworth Castle in England was enormous. It held two hundred enemy soldiers and eleven catapults (rock launchers). Yet belfries weren't foolproof. They were unsteady and could topple over. Castle soldiers would try to set them on fire.

Attackers tried to hide under wheeled shelters, nicknamed "cats," "rats," "tortoises," or "hedgehogs." Defenders pelted these shelters (and the soldiers inside) with huge rocks. They could be crushed like roadkill.

Medieval Missiles

Other methods of attack were set up. A **ballista**, a giant crossbow, was used to fire huge spears at the castle. Castle soldiers would shoot their own crossbows right back. They had the advantage of hiding behind the stone "giant's teeth" and arrow loops in castle walls.

The attackers called in engineers to build wheeled structures called **siege engines**. These were used to launch heavy boulders at the castle. Huge catapults would fling 300-pound rocks, iron balls, or even dead cows. Attackers hoped that rotting animals would spread disease in the castle. As another sickening scare tactic, they would toss over the chopped-off heads of prisoners. Perhaps more terrifying were fire pots. These were clay pots filled with burning tar and oil. When hurled inside the castle, they exploded into fireballs. The fire was almost impossible to put out. To fight back, the castle built its own catapults. Soldiers would fling the enemies' own rocks right back at them. The castle's height was an advantage when lobbing missiles downhill.

Attackers wouldn't give up so easily. They would try to smash down a castle wall or gate using a **battering ram**. This weapon was a huge tree trunk topped with an iron ram's head (or even a real one). The pole was mounted on wheels. It was swung back and forth on leather straps. Soldiers pushing the battering ram were protected by a wooden shelter. Defenders would drop down bundles of burning wood and tar to set the shelter on fire. They used a large hook to throw off the battering ram. They also lowered wooden panels, sacks, or a huge mattress to blunt the blows.

The Big Dig

Another way attackers would try to conquer a castle was by digging under the walls until they collapsed. This tactic was extremely difficult. Attackers would look for the weakest part of a stone wall, one that was poorly defended. They would dig a tunnel. Then they would prop up the stone walls with timber and set the wood on fire. Without support, the walls would crumble.

In 1215, King John of England led a "piggish" attack on a castle in Rochester. His troops dug a tunnel under the corner

of a tower. The digging took more than six weeks. Then the king ordered forty fat pigs to be killed. The dead animals were stuffed inside the tunnel and set on fire. The pig fat burned for hours. Finally, the wall collapsed. King John's soldiers invaded the castle.

Toilet Attack

Sometimes attackers used stinky tricks to invade a castle. During the siege on Chateau Gaillard in 1204, a French soldier had a nasty idea. He and his troops crawled up one by one through the smelly toilet shaft and into the castle! Once inside, they made a lot of noise. The English defenders were tricked into thinking that a huge French force had broken through the castle's outer wall. The English soldiers quickly ran to defend the castle's inner courtyard. Meanwhile, the French soldiers hurried to the gatehouse. They lowered the drawbridge. The French army stormed the castle and won the battle.

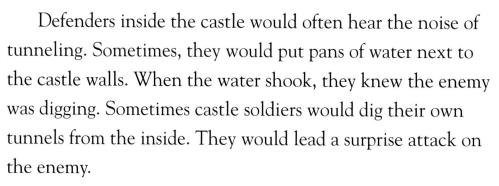

Sometimes these big digs backfired. In 1287, Lord Stafford of England led a siege against a Welsh castle. While he and his men were crawling through one of their tunnels, the roof of the tunnel caved in. The men were buried alive.

Defenders inside the castle would often hear the noise of tunneling. Sometimes, they would put pans of water next to the castle walls. When the water shook, they knew the enemy was digging. Sometimes castle soldiers would dig their own tunnels from the inside. They would lead a surprise attack on the enemy.

Still Standing

Toward the end of the Middle Ages, castles became outdated. They could no longer stand up to the newest explosive weapons—guns and cannons. Instead of being used as fortresses, some castles were turned into mansions or prisons. Others were left to crumble.

By today's standards, castles may not seem like dream homes. Castles were

chaotic. Early castles were dark, damp, and dreary. During a siege, all castles were downright scary. Yet their construction was an amazing feat. Some castles were built so strong that they are still standing today. Many are popular tourist attractions. One of the best examples is Windsor Castle, home to England's Queen Elizabeth II. It stands on the original man-made hill, dating back to 1067. Some of Windsor Castle's stone buildings have survived since 1154.

Can you imagine *any* home today still standing a thousand years from now? Castles of the Middle Ages may have been yucky, but one thing's for certain: They were tough!

Words to Know

arrow loop—A narrow slit cut into a castle wall through which soldiers fired arrows.

ballista—A large crossbow that fired spears.

battering ram—A wooden pole or tree trunk used to smash a castle's wall or gate.

belfry—A tall wooden tower with wheels that was used in attacks on castles.

cesspit—A deep ditch that collects human waste.

crenel—A gap between raised stone notches on top of a castle's walls.

drawbridge—A wooden platform that spanned a moat; it could be raised or lowered to protect the castle.

earthenware—Pottery made of baked, hardened clay.

gatehouse—Guarded entry to the castle.

joust—A contest in which two knights on horseback dueled against each other with lances.

lance—A long wooden weapon with a metal head.

melee—A mock battle in which teams of knights clashed against each other on horseback.

moat—A deep ditch surrounding a castle, sometimes filled with water.

murder hole—A hole cut into the roof of a gatehouse through which defenders poured down boiling liquids, stones, and other missiles on the enemy.

sewage—Liquid and solid human waste (pee and poop).

siege engine—A wooden machine used to hurl stones and other missiles at castle walls.

Further Reading

Adams, Brian. **Medieval Castles.** Mankato, Minn.: Stargazer Books, 2007.

Gravett, Christopher. Castle. New York: DK Publishing, Inc., 2004.

Johnson, Sheri. **Kids in The Medieval World.** Mankato, Minn.: Capstone Press, 2009.

Lassieur, Allison. The Middle Ages: An Interactive History Adventure. Mankato, Minn.: You Choose Books, 2010.

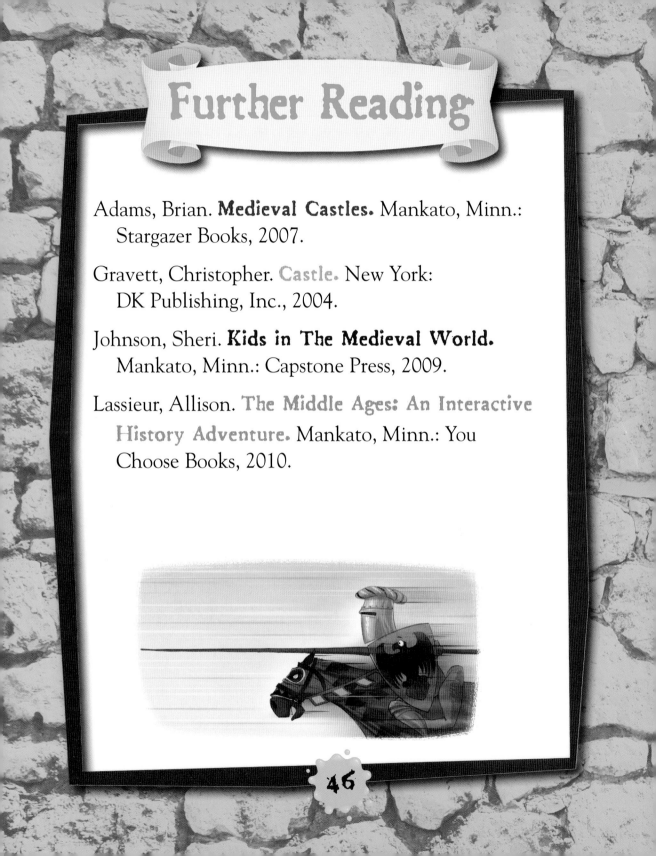

Internet Addresses

PBS. NOVA Online: Destroy the Castle
<http://www.pbs.org/wgbh/nova/lostempires/
trebuchet/destroy.html>

Castles of the World. Castles for Kids
<http://www.castles.org/Kids_Section/Castle_Story/
index.htm>

Kids on the Net. Kids' Castle
<http://www.kidsonthenet.org.uk/castle/view.html>

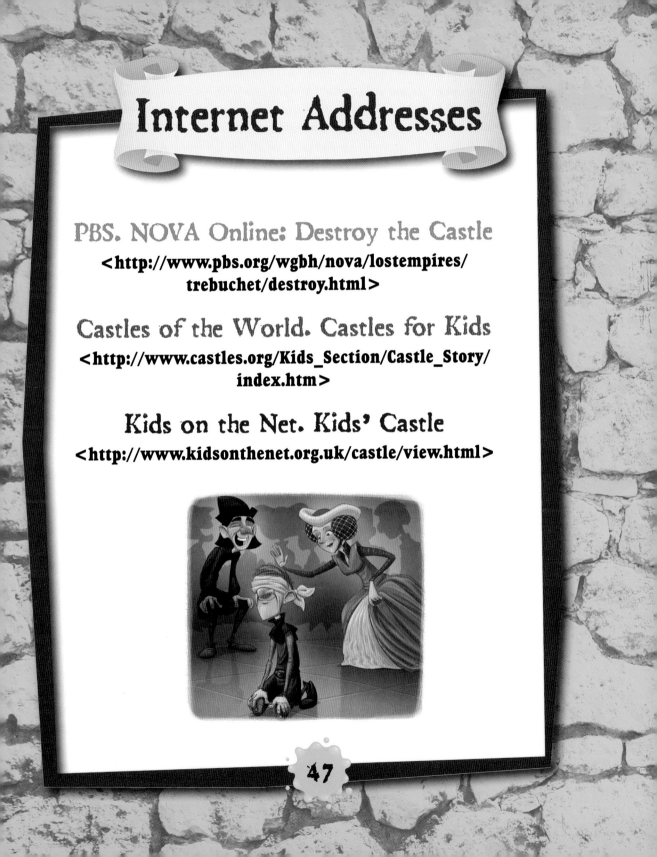

Index